W9-AVW-017

10 Things College Students Need to Know About Money

Shay Olivarria

www.BiggerThanYourBlock.com

Copyright 2010

All rights reserved. No part of this book may be reproduced,
scanned, stored, or distributed in any printed or electronic form
without the written permission of the author.

The author is not an attorney or accountant and cannot offer
professional advice. She suggests you explore these subjects with
competent advisors. She is a frequent speaker and group facilitator
on personal finance related subjects.

You won't be in college forever.

Table of Contents

Foreword

Foreword

Thank you for buying this book. Thank you for being interested in knowing more about personal finance. Thank you for being proactive.

I wrote this book because I was angry. I made quite a few mistakes with money in my youth because I didn't know any better. No one in my family, neighborhood, or school taught me about managing my money. When I got my first job at 16 I spent most of my money on clothes and food. I now know that:

> ➤ I wasted thousands of dollars on depreciating assets.
> ➤ If I would have invested even a fourth of what I earned I would have created good savings habits earlier and I would have amassed a tidy sum of money.
> ➤ I would have become more confident earlier on if I had taken an interest in finding out what I didn't know.

I wrote this book so that you won't make the same mistakes I did.

Thank you to everyone that contributed anything to the making of this book. Thank you to the nephews, godkids, and cousins in my life that motivate me to continue this work. Thank you to all the youth that I've worked with across the US. Knowing I'm helping you makes everything worthwhile. Thank you to my family and friends that have supported me from day one. You know all the love and suggestions you've provided over the years.

Especially, thank you to my husband who has gone above and beyond in every area that matters. He is the strongest man I know. I am honored that he has chosen to spend his life with me.

PEACE,
Shay Olivarria
The most dynamic financial education speaker working today

Chapter One

The world is Bigger Than Your Block
Why looking at the big picture is important

> ➢ You can't make good choices if you don't understand what's at stake
> ➢ Personal finance is more than income
> ➢ Think value not cost

You're reading this book because you want to know more about personal finance. That's awesome! The first place to start is at the beginning. The first step in feeling powerful in regard to your finances is to understand exactly where you stand.

It doesn't matter how much money you have or how little money you have. If you don't take the time to think about the bigger picture you won't get too far. Looking at the bigger picture includes understanding where you stand financially, thinking about your financial situation as more than your income, and buying based on value not cost.

<u>You can't make good choices if you don't understand what's at stake.</u>

The very first thing you'll have to start with is taking a brutally honest look at where you stand financially. This is no time to play games and lie to your self. You'll have to decide if you truly want to control your finances and make your money work for you or if you're okay with always putting out financial fires and never being secure financially. The choice is yours.

When you're young you tend to not see the whole equation and not understand how much what you do today will affect you later, so let's use an example. Let's say you got a job when you were sixteen years old and you started saving $150 a month and you saved only the same $150 every month from sixteen to sixty-five, assuming you earned an average 8% interest rate, you'd have earned $1,104,165.70. Guess what the most beautiful part of this equation is? Out of a little more than $1.1M you will only have contributed $88,200. Yes, you read that correctly. That means that you will input a small amount and get 12.5 times what you put in through the Magic of Compound Interest.

To contrast how important it is for you to start managing your money effectively *now*, let's see another example. If you wait until you're twenty-one years old to start contributing you'll only earn $733,680.46. By waiting five years you will have lost $370,485. It gets worse. Wait until you're thirty years old and your savings will shrink to $346,376.25.

That doesn't mean that if you haven't begun aggressively saving your money it's too late. It does mean that you're losing thousands of dollars in compound interest by choosing to waste your money on small expenses like eating out, buying snacks from vending machines, and treating your friends to lunch.

Personal finance is more than income

If you can't think past how much money you're earning you may as well put this book down right now. It makes no sense to base your idea of how well you're doing off of your income without considering your expenses. I'll say it again, "it makes no sense".

How many of us have heard about famous people, rich people that have gone broke? It doesn't matter whether you're earning $18,000 a year or $250,000 if you don't have the knowledge *and the will* to manage your money, you will end up broke. End of story.

There are endless stories of people that worked at average, blue collar jobs all their lives and managed to buy a house, put several kids through college, and some even ended up with enough money in retirement to make large donations to causes they cared about. It's not how much you make, it's how much you spend.

To find out where you stand financially you have to take into account not only your income (earnings, student financial aid, social security income, etc.), but also your expenses (housing, utilities, gas, auto loans, credit card bills, etc.). Think about how many times you've gotten paid on Friday and by Monday you have no idea where the money went. All those expenditures are what's keeping you from mastering your money.

<u>Think value not cost</u>

It may not seem like it, but there is a difference between "value" and "cost". Let me explain. Let's say you have to buy a new pair of shoes. You have a few options:

a) You buy a new pair from your local big-box chain for around $40.
b) You buy a new pair from your local shopping center for around $90.
c) You buy a new pair from your local upscale boutique and spend around $185.

With option A the cost is low, and the value is moderate. They'll do the job …. For a while. With option B the cost is moderate and the value is good. Most moderately priced shoes are made sufficiently and will do the job for a long while. With option C the cost is high and many times the value is good. Many higher end brands are made of good quality material and will do the job for a long while.

The conversation around "cost" and "value" really becomes a decision around balance. In a perfect world you'd want a good product at a good price. Usually you'll have to negotiate in one of those areas. My experience with cheap shoes tells me that they are usually not well made so they hurt my feet and become worn out a bit faster than their more expensive counter parts. The super expensive shoes are usually more money than I'm willing to part with, but they usually fit me pretty well. Usually, they fit me as well as the more moderately priced shoes. I'm sure you can see where I'm going with this. I tend to buy in the middle. I'd rather buy one pair of moderately priced shoes that fit me well and will last for a while than a cheap pair that I'll have to replace sooner (thereby costing me more money) or an expensive pair that will cost me twice as much and end up feeling the same as the moderately priced pair.

Short version: cheaper isn't always better. Know *why* you're buying, *what* you're buying, and look for the key things that you need. Shop smarter and look for value.

In conclusion, whether you spend your life making excuses and jumping from one financial setback to another or making your money work for you and feeling powerful it is up to you. Remember that the first step in mastering your money is to understand where you're starting from and making good decisions based on the big picture.

Tips
  ➤ Start thinking about persona finance as more than just income.
  ➤ Know the difference between cost and value.

Shay Olivarria

Chapter Two

That's My Attitude
How your money attitude influences your behavior

- ➤ Recognize that how you feel about money motivates your behavior
- ➤ Value yourself enough to be responsible with your money
- ➤ Invest in yourself every month

I'm sure you've heard it said before, "Attitude affects everything" well, money is no exception. Until we understand why we have the habits we have and how we came to have those habits we won't change. It's that simple. The first step is to recognize that how we feel about money motivates our behavior. The second step is to value yourself enough to be responsible with your money. Lastly, you'll have to invest in yourself.

How many times have you purchased something you didn't even really want because you wanted to feel good? How many times have you felt pressure to buy something because your friends were there and you didn't want to look cheap? How many times have you gone out of your way to save a few extra dollars only to realize at the end of the adventure that you saved a few dollars, but those dollars were not worth all the trouble you went through to save the few dollars?

It doesn't matter if you spend too much or are too frugal. Unless you understand why you feel the way you do about using money you won't be able to find balance.

Recognize how you feel about money motivates your behavior

The first step in changing any behavior is recognizing that behavior. Many people don't really take the time to sit down and think about why they do the things that they do. Let's take a moment and really think this through. Answer each question honestly, even if only to yourself:

1) Growing up, my parent(s) seemed _____ about money.
2) Growing up, a phrase I heard often about money was _____.
3) My first job was _____. I used the money to _____.
4) When I thought about the costs involved with college, I thought I would pay for them by _____.
5) When I'm with friends I feel _____ about money.
6) When I think about managing my money I feel _____.
7) The thing that concerns me most about money is _____.
8) This amount of money in my bank account would make me feel great _____.

9) I have that much money now or I'm working towards that goal. Why or why not?

<u>Value yourself enough to be responsible with your money</u>

How you spend your money is a direct reflection of how you feel about yourself. When you feel secure in who you are you don't need to be flashy with your money or try to impress others with what you have, or want them to *think* you have.

When you value yourself you want to take care of yourself. You want to use your money in a way that enables you to feel good, safe, and secure. Knowing that you have enough money to pay your bills, enough to have emergency money in case something comes up, and enough stashed away for retirement gives one a sense of power.

On the other hand, wasting your money shows that you don't care about yourself and you don't care about your future. When everything's going well you'll have plenty of friends to hang out with and the money runs out you'll be alone. <u>People don't value people that don't value themselves.</u> If you carry yourself in a way that tells people that your life, your money, and your future is not important then that is the way people will treat you. How many times have you seen people treat others that way? How many times have you treated someone in a less-than-respectful way because that's how they carried themselves?

Invest in yourself every month

I'm about to say something that might surprise you. You, person reading this book, are a business. You are the business of Me, Inc. and it is your job to make sure that you're business is running "in the black", that means with no deficits. Like any business you have income and you have expenses. There are some expenses that *must* be paid on time, every time and there are some expenses that have a little bit of leeway. Most of us run Me, Inc. by putting our immediate living expenses in the must-be-paid category and everything else in the it'll-get-done-when-it-gets-done category. The problem with this thinking is that we usually aren't putting the right things in the right categories.

Putting money away for your emergency fund and for your retirement should be priority number one. If you pay all your other expenses and put your future last on the list there will never be enough money left over to save. When you spend money, you're investing in whatever company owns that fast-food chain, whatever manufacturer makes those shoes, and whatever company sold you that music. You're investing in things all day long. Why not invest in yourself?

What we usually do is look at our income and pay our most pressing bills. After that we have that I-worked-all-week-and-I-have-nothing-to-show-for-it feeling so we take whatever money we have left and blow it on something that will make us feel better. For some it's a full priced movie replete with $5 drink and $8 nachos. For some it's a new outfit. For some it's a trip out with your friends. Whatever it is, that's money that could have been put toward your future. You might enjoy spending $50 right now, but it could have grown to $1,669.60 if it was put into a retirement savings account and left to grow for forty-four years. Let that sink in. The $50 you spend today could grow to $1,669.60. That's one purchase. Imagine if you thought about how much each of your miscellaneous expenses cost and how much money they would be worth in the future. How much money do you think you've spent on things you didn't need, and maybe didn't even really want? It starts to mess with your mind a bit, no?

Now, let's be clear: I'm not saying that you should never spend a penny on enjoying yourself in the here and now. What I am saying is that I want you spend money with your eyes wide open. If you want to spend all your money then feel free to do that, but don't complain about how life isn't fair and you don't make enough money and blah, blah, blah. Spend, but spend wisely. Investing in your self is the best way to spend.

<u>Pay yourself first</u>

The very first person you should be thinking about every time you get paid is yourself! You should put away money in your emergency account and your retirement account before you pay anyone else. All your financial obligations (rent, vacations, debt, etc.) should be adjusted to fit your spending plan *after* you've put money away in your emergency account and your retirement account. Got it?

No one is going to be there to bail you out when your tire blows on the expressway or your sixty-seven years old and haven't saved a dime. It's up to you to make sure that you have money available to take care of yourself. Show personal pride by making sure that you are putting money away in your emergency account and retirement account.

Don't forget: emergency account and retirement account. Say it with me! Emergency account and retirement account. Nice!

Tips

- ➢ Think about how you saw money being used in your youth.
- ➢ Try to connect specific instances that you saw to feelings that you have about money now.
- ➢ Show that you value yourself by making wise choices about personal finance.
- ➢ Pay yourself first every month.

Chapter Three

Know your (financial) worth
What net worth is and why it's important

- ➤ What is net worth?
- ➤ How do you calculate your net worth?

I'm sure you've heard the saying, "how do you expect to get where you're going if you don't have a map". This saying has never been truer than when dealing with money. In this case your map is your net worth.

What is net worth?

Net worth is a number that tells you your true financial value. Too many times we define our financial value in terms of income; however this is not a true representation. Listing all your assets and subtracting that number from all your liabilities is the only way to know what financial footing you're on.

Most people couldn't tell you how much total debt they have or how much value they have in assets. In fact, if you were to ask someone what they thought their financial worth was right this second, I bet you they would laugh and mention something about their income.

How do you calculate your net worth?

It's not how much you earn it's how much you spend that matters. We have all heard of people that make $100,000 a year and spend $120,000. Heck, I'll take it a step forward and say we've all heard about people that bring in $10M a year and spend $10.5M. Haven't we all said, "If I was that rich, I would never go broke"?

Think about all the assets that you have. An asset is something valuable. Think cars, homes, investment accounts, cash, high end jewelry, etc. Make a list that includes each thing and it's approximate value. You're going to subtract your liabilities from this number.

Liabilities are amounts of money that you owe. Think college loans, car loans, home loans, credit card debt, monies owed to family and friends, etc. Make a list that includes all the liabilities that you owe. To get a fair assessment it's imperative that you include every debt you can think of.

Total Assets
- Total Liabilities
_____

Net Worth

If you're looking for an easy net worth worksheet, check out the one in *Money Matters: The Get It Done in 1 Minute Workbook*. How do I know it's an awesome worksheet? For starters, I wrote it and everything I do is awesome! Is that too much? Oh well. Check out the net worth worksheet and tell me what you think.

Tips

> Include current approximate value of assets. Just because you paid a certain amount for something doesn't mean that it's worth that amount now.
> Include *all* debt owed. That includes loans from family and friends as well as credit cards, student loans and other debts.

Chapter Four

It's all the same. Or is it?

Differences between a bank and a credit union and why it matters

- ➤ What are the benefits of using a financial institution?
- ➤ A bank is a financial institution that exists to make money for it's shareholders.
- ➤ A credit union is a financial institution that exists to help shareholders have access to financial services.

Over the years many people have asked me why I'm so keen on credit unions. My answers are usually full of emotion. For example, I like that the staff at my credit union know me by name and I can call and speak to a knowledgeable person during business hours. I like that I earn a good rate of interest, which gives me more money, at my credit union than I would get at a traditional bank. Just to show that I'm not all bad, I'm going to give you both sides of the topic so you can make an informed decision.

What are the benefits of using a financial institution?

The first thing that we have to talk about is why using a financial institution is a good choice. Some of us may have heard negative things about using financial service institutions. Some of us know people that don't use banks or credit unions and have encouraged us not to use them as well. Some of us are worried about not being able to access the money if it's in a bank. Regardless of the possible reasons against there are four great reasons to use a financial institution:

1) You will earn interest (free money) on your accounts. The amount of interest will change based on which type of account you have, how much money you have in the account and what the going rate is.
2) You will create a relationship that you can use to secure loans and ask for help when you need it.
3) Not carrying large amounts of cash means that you won't lose your money in a robbery or forgot where you put it.
4) Both banks and credit unions are insured by the Federal Deposit Insurance Corporation (FDIC). That means that your money is secure when you put it in a financial institution. If the credit union or bank that you have your money in fails, you're accounts are insured which means you'll still be able to get your money.

A bank is a financial institution that exists to make money for its shareholders.

Almost everyone knows what a bank is and what its function is, but let's make sure we're all starting from the same point. Banks are financial institutions that provide a way for individuals and businesses to cash checks, write checks, and have access to savings accounts such as general savings accounts, Certificates of Deposits (CDs), and Money Market Accounts. The American Bankers Association (ABA) 2004 Bank Marketing Survey found that banks spent $9.4 billion, yes that's with a "b", on marketing in 2004.

Banks spend that kind of money on marketing because they want you, the customer, to know what products and services they offer and view them as trustworthy enough for you to bank with them. That's all fine, well, and good as long as you keep one thing in mind: banks are for profit. At the end of the day the bank is responsible for making a profit for their shareholders.

There's nothing wrong with businesses making a profit, however I want to be clear that no matter what banks say, they are not there to be your friend or help you out. At best, they are a financial institution that you can partner with to take care of your banking needs. At worst, they are a business that is set up to take advantage of your lack of knowledge and experience. Each bank is its own business and each one has different processes and strategies to serve customers.

Realize that as a for-profit business the first concern of banks are their shareholders. If serving customers well will help banks earn more money, then they will do that. If treating customers poorly will help banks earn more money, then they will do that too. When you're dealing with a financial institution, treat that institution as if it's a professional resource. Don't assume that the bank will do whatever is in your best interest.

<u>A credit union is a financial institution that exists to help shareholders have access to financial services.</u>

Credit unions do everything that banks do with one exception: credit unions are *not* for profit. A credit union is formed when people that have something in common band together to create a financial institution. Wikipedia defines credit unions as:

> "a cooperative financial institution that is owned and controlled by its members, and operated for the purpose of promoting thrift, providing credit at reasonable rates, and providing other financial services to its members."

In plain terms, a group of people that live in the same area, go to the same school, work at the same job, attend the same church, etc. pool their money together to loan money to each other and provide a financial institution framework. Any way you cut it, it's cooperative economics. You have a voice. You have a choice.

Credit unions are available in every state in the United States and most foreign countries. You can find out more about credit unions by visiting www.CreditUnion.coop. They offer better loan rates, and usually, better customer service because each person that has an account at the credit union owns a portion of the credit union.

It's imperative that you have access to a bank or credit union for financial services. Remember that a bank is not your only choice. Find a financial institution that provides the products and services you need and is willing to partner with you to have a positive experience.

Tips

> ➤ The only stupid question is the one you don't ask. If they don't want to answer your questions then they don't need your business.
> ➤ Find a financial institution that offers the products and services that you need.
> ➤ Use a financial institution that is willing to explain their fee schedule until you understand it.
> ➤ Find a financial institution that has employees that you can speak with whenever you have a question.

Shay Olivarria

Chapter Five

Make your money work for you
Differences between financial accounts

- ➢ Savings accounts
- ➢ Certificate of Deposit (CD)
- ➢ Money Market Account (MMA)

There is no reason that you need to be beholden to your money. In fact, your money should be working hard for you even when you're sleeping. In this chapter we'll explore three different accounts that are available to help you save your money: savings accounts, Certificates of Deposit, and Money Market Accounts.

Savings Accounts

I'm sure we've all heard of the term "savings account". The term is generally used for accounts that are offered by financial institutions that help you save money. They differ from checking accounts because they don't provide an option to write checks. The accounts offered by most financial institutions are easily accessible; however they offer very low interest rates.

Ask anyone you know how much money they have managed to save using a savings account and I'll bet most of those people will tell you that they haven't saved much. The reason is simple: it's too easy to take your money out and you don't earn a whole lot of interest even when your money stays in the account.

There are a few other options that are great ways to keep your money available and earn a better rate of interest than savings accounts. Two are mentioned below.

Certificates of Deposit (CD)

Certificates of Deposit are basically loans that you give the bank in exchange for an agreed upon rate of interest. Typically, there are Certificates of Deposit for time spans that are as short as 7 days and as long as 2 years, or more. You get to choose how long you want to loan the bank your money. How much interest is earned depends on how long you loan the bank your money. Although CDs sound great so far, a word of caution needs to be mentioned. If you agree to loan the bank your money for a specific amount of time and you change your mind, you can get your money back but you'll have to forfeit part of your earned interest.

Let's make sure this point is clear: Certificates of Deposit are an agreement between you and the bank. If you choose not to honor that agreement, the bank will take some of the interest you would have earned. You will not lose your principle. CDs should be used as part of a financial strategy to make your money work for you.

CD laddering is a strategy where the customer sets up each Certificate of Deposit to mature at a specific month in a pattern that allows CDs to mature and be re-invested so that each month, year, or whatever time table you want to set up, CDs are maturing. For example, I can set up CDs to mature every month if I choose a 90 day CD (typically, the longer you leave the money in the CD the more interest you will earn) and buy one every month. This way I'll have access to a higher rate of interest by choosing a longer time for the CD to mature, but I'll also have a CD maturing every month after the third month because I bought one every month.

Money Market Account (MMA)

A Money Market Account is a type of hybrid checking and savings account. It functions like a checking account because you can make deposits and withdrawals by check, teller or by ATM card, however it acts like a restrictive savings account because you are only allowed to make a certain amount of deposits and withdrawals per month. In exchange for these restrictions you earn a higher interest rate.

MMAs are great accounts to use for emergency funds. They are liquid, easily accessible, and have a higher rate of interest than a regular savings account. All financial institutions, banks and credit unions, offer them to customers.

Good changes to fees

In 2010 the CARD Act went into effect and changes many aspects of personal finance for Americans. A couple of these changes include:

- Customers have the option to "opt-in" to over limit coverage instead of having a bank cover any overages and charge you a fee for the convenience. If customers choose to have this coverage an over limit fee can only be applied once per billing cycle instead of once for every instance.
- Banks cannot charge you to pay your bill by mail, online, telephone, etc. unless it's an expedited payment.

At the end of the day it's up to you to choose which account is the best fit for your financial situation and savings habits.

Tips
- ➢ Choose an account based on how quickly you'll need to be able to access the money.
- ➢ Find out what the going interest rates are on savings accounts, Certificates of Deposit, and Money Market Accounts at different financial institutions by looking online or in newspapers.

Chapter Six

Credit is king!
What's a FICO score and why is it important?

> What's a FICO score?
> The 5 things that affect your credit score the most
> How the CARD Act might effect you
> Why credit scores are important
> How to get your reports and/or scores
> What to do if something is wrong.

What's a FICO score?

A FICO score is the numerical representation of your credit worthiness that ranges between 300 and 850. It's a complex algorithm that takes into account several aspects of your financial behavior and let's lenders know how you might handle paying back any loans they give you.

There are three major credit scoring agencies in the United States: Experian, TransUnion, and Equifax. Each of them has a separate file on you and because of that, each of them has a separate score for you. That's right you have 3 credit scores and all of them may be different.

What happens is different lenders contract with different agencies to report your credit history. Some of them contract with only one and some of them contract with all three.

The 5 things that affect your credit score the most

Though the FICO scoring system takes into account many different aspects of your financial behavior there are 5 major components of the scoring system. The good part is you control the most important aspects with your choices:

Length of credit – how long you've had a credit file. Generally, the longer you've had a credit file the better. It's easier to predict your behavior if you been managing credit for a good while.

Types of credit – there are two basic types of credit that lenders want to see you manage: revolving accounts and installment accounts. Revolving accounts are accounts that increase or decrease due to your purchases. For example, a credit card and a store charge card are both revolving accounts. Installment accounts are accounts that have a set principle, a set amount of interest, and set payments. For example, a mortgage and a car loan are both installment accounts.

Debt ratio – this is how much credit has been extended to you versus how much you've already used. For example, let's say you have a credit card with a $1,000 limit and you've already charged $700. Take what you've charged ($700) and divide that number by the amount of credit you have been extended ($1,000) and you'll get your debt ratio of .70 or 70%. If you have more than one credit card, add all the debt accrued and divide it by all the credit extended to get the debt ratio. Lenders want to see your debt ratio under 30%.

Payment history – lenders want to know if you've been paying your bills on time. Your credit report will show bills as being paid, 30 days late, 60 days late, 90 days late, or written off. Obviously, you want to pay your bills on time so that this area will be a positive on your credit report and scores.

Credit inquiries – how many times in recent history you've applied for credit. These are sometimes called, "hard inquiries". These are inquiries initiated by a third party, whoever you've applied for credit with, for a new service or loan. They will stay on your credit report for two years. The more times you applied for credit the worse it looks. Creditors may wonder why you're trying to open so many accounts.

"Soft inquiries" are initiated by you. You are allowed to look at your reports and/or scores as much as you like without any negative consequences.

How the CARD Act might affect you

In 2009 the average American college student graduated with a little over $3,000 in credit card debt. College students were sometimes preyed upon by credit card companies because many students didn't understand how credit worked. The credit card companies would show up on campus and offer students small gifts like Frisbees or t-shirts to apply for credit cards with high interest rates. For these reasons, the CARD Act was passed in 2009 and started functioning in February of 2010.

The CARD Act has created some major changes in personal finance. Let's take a look at what I think is the largest one to affect college students. No one under the age of 21 will be able to get a credit card unless a) they can prove that they have sufficient income to pay for a credit card or b) they have a co-signer over the age of 21.

There is some debate over how this will really affect college students. Some argue that parents will co-sign for cards for students. Some argue that students without strong familial support will be without a crucial back-up plan. How the CARD Act will mean to you is obviously dependent upon your situation.

Why are credit scores important?

Keeping you credit report error free and credit scores high are important because:

- Many jobs are now checking credit scores before they hire you.
- Credit scores are used to determine everything from if you can get a cell phone to if you'll be able to rent an apartment.

- The loan rates that you are charged for auto loans, home loans, etc. depend on your credit score.

I can't stress the importance of monitoring your credit score enough. The usual argument I hear from students is that they don't use credit, so credit scores don't matter. I beg to differ. Your credit scores are going to be looked at when you apply for an apartment, when you need to have your electricity, gas, cable, etc. turned on, and when you apply for a job. If you use money, you're going to need to have a good credit score.

How to get your reports and/or scores

It's really simple to get your credit reports and/or scores online. You just create an account, log on, and wait a few seconds for your reports and/or scores to pop up on the screen.

There is only one site that allows you to order your credit reports for free: www.AnnualCreditReport.com. This is the *only* site that you can order your credit reports from Experian, TransUnion, and Equifax for free once a year. Nope, you can't get them for free on that site. I know the one you're thinking of. Not that one either. Those other sites give you your credit report for free after you sign up for monthly credit monitoring. That's not really free.

You can also pay for your credit reports and scores. It will cost about $40 for all three reports and scores. Each company has their own algorithm, so each score may be different. The only way to see the scores is to buy them.

<u>What to do if something is wrong.</u>

If you order your reports and/or scores and you realize that information is incorrect or you've had your identity stolen contact each credit bureau individually (by internet, phone or mail) and let them know what's happened. They may ask for more information to clear it up, but it a pretty simple, straight-forward, free process. Do not pay anyone to "fix" your credit. All they are doing is writing letters on your behalf. You can do that for free.

Tips

> Check your credit report and score at least once a year. You can pull reports, not scores, from www.AnnualCreditReport.com for free once a year.
> Make sure all the information on your report is correct including addresses, names, jobs, etc.
> Checking your own credit report and/or score will not lower your score.
> Check your score before you apply for a loan. That way you can get a ballpark estimate and make sure you're getting a good rate.

Chapter Seven

Fake money with real interest rates
How credit cards work

- ➢ The psychology of credit cards
- ➢ How the CARD Act changes the credit card rules

Credit cards are a great tool to have in your personal finance arsenal, but there is good and bad in everything. Credit cards are good to have when you travel because the credit card company acts as protection against loss, however they are also a huge temptation to spend more than you can easily pay off. There's a psychological component to all the hype about credit cards that helps people spend more than they can pay off. There is also a structural component that is set up to help credit card users stay in debt. The CARD Act has set some new guidelines for credit card companies that should help with some of those structural issues.

The psychology of credit cards

I'm sure we all know, or have heard of, people that have gotten in over their heads with credit cards. Some of the blame lies with the behavior of the card holder. There's something psychological about being able to slide a card and buy things. You don't feel the same as you would if you had paid cash. The same is true of debit cards. Try it some time. Instead of using your debit or credit card to buy something, go to the bank, withdraw the cash you'll need, and buy the products or services with cash. I bet it'll be harder for you to fork over that stack of twenty dollar bills than it would have been to slide that card. There's a reason that card issuers want you to "slide" or "tap" instead of "pay" for things.

How the CARD Act changes the credit card rules

In February of 2010 the Obama administration's CARD Act went into effect to protect credit card consumers. There are several new pieces to the act, however the 6 things that will affect the average college students are noted below.

- No one under 21 years old will be able to have a credit card unless they a) can prove that they can pay for the card or b) they have a co-signer.
- All payments over the minimum must be applied to the purchases with the highest interest rates first. This will help you pay off your credit card bill sooner if you stick to the plan and pay more than the minimum payment every month.
- Payments will be due on the same day of the month every month. No more worries or guesses about what day your credit card bill will be due. This should make it a little easier to stick to a plan to pay off your card(s).
- Customers have to be mailed statements at least 21 days before the due date.

Although the CARD Act has helped to protect credit card users, at the end of the day it's up to you to choose a card that meets your needs and be responsible about its usage.

Credit cards aren't magic money that you don't have to pay back. They are very serious business and their misuse has driven plenty of folks to bankruptcy. Now that many college students will depend on parents, grandparents, or other potential co-signers it's going to be even more important to handle credit cards responsibly. Your behavior is going to affect whoever co-signed for your credit card. If you choose not to pay back the money you owe, the creditor will go after whoever co-signed the loan, aggressively.

The last thing you want is to make a close relationship feel uncomfortable over a few pizzas and pairs of shoes. They trusted you to be responsible with their credit reputation. It's up to you to prove that they did the right thing.

Tips
- ➤ Read all the small type in the credit card offer.
- ➤ Know what the interest rate is.
- ➤ Think about how long it will take you to pay off what you charge, not only the principle but the interest as well.

Shay Olivarria

Chapter Eight

You use money, don't you?
Why you must have a spending plan

➢ Irrefutable proof that you need a spending plan
➢ How to create a spending plan

One of the most common things I hear from college students is that they don't make spending plans because they don't need them. My response? If you use money you need a plan to use it efficiently. We all spend money. The question is: are we using it to our best benefit? For many of us the answer to that question is, "no".

Irrefutable proof that you need a spending plan

Have you ever pulled a $20 out of the ATM and two hours later you have no idea how you spent the money? If you answered, "yes" that's why you need a spending plan. Most of us spend small amounts of money everyday on things that we don't event remember buying. That $1 soda at work takes up $240 a year. How many times have you walked into a store to grab 1 thing and come out more than you intended?

How to create a spending plan

Having a spending plan is a way to help you recognize what you've been spending your money on and what changes you may want to make. It's simple to make a spending plan using 7 easy steps:

1) Go through your bank statements and credit card statements. Put the money you spent in categories so you can see what you spent your money on. There is nothing like seeing where your money is going in black and white. Once you realize that you're spending $400 on fast food it might help you make some changes. I like to use personal finance software programs because you can download your bank statements right into the program and assign each expenditure to a category. It's really easy and quick. Notice all the money that you spent on non-essential items and move on to step number two.

2) Don't freak out when you see how much money you waste every month. We all spend money in ways that are unwise and we all deserve to have a little "mad money" every month, however I bet you don't realize just how much money you're wasting every month. Again, don't freak out. Breathe.

3) Make a list of your fixed expenses; the bills that you have to pay every month. For example, your rent/mortgage, lights, water, gas, car insurance, credit cards, etc.

4) Make a list of your variable expenses; the bills that you may have to pay an increase or decrease based on your behavior. For example, the payment for your credit cards, your quarterly tax payments if you're self employed, etc.

5) Make a line on your list that says, "My Emergency Fund". You are going to start paying yourself every month just like you pay everyone else. Creating, or adding to, an emergency fund is one of the main reasons you need a spending plan. Take all that money you've been wasting and put it into an account that you can use when you're in a jam. I suggest trying to build up 6 – 12 month's worth of income. When an emergency comes, and there will always be an emergency, you'll be ready.

6) Make a line that says, "Retirement". I don't care if you haven't even opened a retirement account yet or you can only put $5 in it. You're going to start putting money aside for your old age. As your money market account swells with cash you can take time to think about where you'd like to invest it. The first step is to start. You must start investing for your retirement. The more you put away now, the less you'll have to worry later. If you start saving $50 a month and earn an average interest rate of 8% you'll accrue $243,649.31 by the time you're 65 years old. The best part of this equation is that because of compound interest you'll only have put in $27,000.00 and the rest will be interest. Not too bad, right? Think about if you saved $100 a month. What if you saved

$200 a month? Compound interest will make a huge difference in your retirement lifestyle. Start now.

7) Whatever money you have left, go wild! You know what your fixed expenses will cost every month, what your upcoming variable expenses will be, you've put money away for your emergency fund, and you're started contributing to your retirement account. The money left over is called your "discretionary income". Take this money and enjoy yourself knowing that you're doing everything you need to be doing to become, or stay, financially stable.

If you find that you don't have enough income to cover all your expenses listed on your spending plan, then you have two choices. You're going to have to increase your income or reduce your expenses and no, cutting out saving for your emergency fund and/or your retirement fund are not options.

If you're looking for a simple worksheet to write down your spending plan, check out the one in Money Matters: The Get It Done in 1 Minute Workbook. You see how I keep mentioning it? You should definitely get it.

Anyhoo ... you are responsible for your life. You have the power to be financially stable or not, by making smart choices.

That's why you need a spending plan.

Tips

> ➢ Know how much you bring in and how you're spending it.
> ➢ Be proactive and make a plan for spending your money so you can use it for the best benefit.
> ➢ You will make money and spend money regardless of if you plan for it or not. Be smart. Make your money work for you.

Shay Olivarria

Chapter Nine

You'll be old one day
How retirement accounts work and why you need to open one now

- ➤ What retirement accounts are
- ➤ Why you need a retirement account
- ➤ Types of retirement accounts
- ➤ How to choose a retirement account
- ➤ How to open a retirement account
- ➤ How to close or change your account

What retirement accounts are

Retirement accounts are investment accounts that have special tax rules to help people save for retirement. Those special tax rules allow people to contribute money that doesn't get taxed the way other dollars do. Those same tax rules also encourage you to keep your money in those retirement accounts until your 59 ½ years old. When I say "encourage" I mean that you can take the money out whenever you want, however depending on your account type there might be a penalty for early withdrawal.

To be clear, when I say, "retirement account" or "mutual fund" I mean a retirement account that invests in mutual funds. There are banks and other financial institutions that will sell you an Individual Retirement Account (IRA) product that does not invest in mutual funds. I am not talking about these accounts. <u>Without investing in mutual funds, an IRA is little more than a savings account.</u>

Having an IRA that invests in a mutual fund is important because it's a safer way to play the stock market. A mutual fund is an account managed by a professional that invests in several stocks and several bonds. The box below represents a mutual fund.

Bonds	Stocks
Tax free bonds	Foreign stocks
Municipal bonds	Domestic Growth stocks

When you invest in a mutual fund you're investing in a bunch of stocks and bonds. Usually, when bonds aren't making money stocks are and stocks aren't making good money bonds are. Investing in both allows you to have less chance of losing your money.

Why you need a retirement account

I don't know about you, but I don't want to work for the rest of my life. How much money do you think you would need to be able to retire? Let's assume that you, the reader, is about twenty years old. Most people will work until they are sixty-five years old (full retirement age is now 67 years old). That means you have forty-five years to save. If you can save $200 a month you'll have $1.1 million dollars, if you earn 9% interest on average. That's only $6.33 a day. That's one fast food meal or movie ticket.

Don't think you can count on social security either. I used the online social security payment estimator to find out how much money per month a person born in 1988 and earning $24,000 per year could expect to receive. The online tool estimated $1,167.00 per month. The web address for the payment estimator can be found in the Resources section of this book. That may seem like a lot, but when you consider all the expenses you'll have as a retired individual I don't think it's enough to live on.

Types of retirement accounts

There are two general types of retirement accounts: those offered from your job (401k/403b) and those that you open without help from your job (Individual Retirement Accounts IRA). Both types have many similarities. Where it gets complicated is that both general types offer both Traditional and Roth options. The most important things to remember are:

- All the money that you save in a retirement account is yours and you can have access to it pretty easily when you want it.
- Setting your retirement account up to have money transferred from your checking account to your retirement account is the easiest way to make sure you're saving money every month.
- Most funds will let you invest with only $50 a month if you agree to invest the $50 every month directly from your checking account.
- The goal of a retirement account is to save for retirement. Don't take the money out. Let it grow over time.
- Choose a no-load mutual fund account. It doesn't matter which one. Studies show that over time almost all funds perform about the same. Don't be overwhelmed by the choices.
- Find a mutual fund that has a low expense ratio. That's where most of your money will get eaten up. 1% is pretty standard. Anything less than 1% is awesome.

Let's take a look at the two most common accounts.

Type of Account	Employer Sponsored		Non-employer Sponsored	
Name of Account	401k/403b		Individual Retirement Accounts (IRA)	
Sub Account	Traditional	Roth	Traditional	Roth
Matching?	Yes	Yes	No	No
When can you take money out without penalty?	59 ½	59 ½	59 ½	59 ½
When do you have to take money out?	70 ½	None	70 ½	None
When do you pay taxes?	When you take the money out.	Before you put the money in.	When you take the money out.	Before you put the money in.
How much can you saver per year?	$16,500	$16,500	$5,000	$5,000
Notes		Principle can be taken out any time without penalty.		Principle can be taken out any time without penalty.

I am not a tax professional or an investment banker. There are tons of rules about retirement accounts, if you want specific advice please consult your financial advisor. The information provided is meant to be an introduction and overview to retirement accounts.

My hope is that you will read this information and want to know more. You're best bet would be to find a fee-only financial advisor. You pay a fee upfront to get help with a specific topic. Since they are not being paid from selling products to you, they have no reason to be biased.

You can find a fee-only financial advisor by visiting the National Association of Personal Financial Advisors (NAPFA) site, clicking on the "Advanced Search" option, entering your zip code, and choosing the "Hourly Financial Planning Services" button. The web address is located in the Resources section at the end of this book.

How to choose a retirement account

Like almost everything in life currently, the best place to find a brokerage to open a retirement account is online. Google "retirement accounts" or "mutual fund brokerage" and you'll see how many different companies come up. Take a look at their sites, read up on different accounts, and make notes about things you have questions about. Request a copy of a prospectus from each account that interests you.

Don't worry so much about which account you choose as long as you feel comfortable calling and speaking with the customer service representatives, feel comfortable using the website, make sure to choose a no-load account, and make sure that the account fees are 1% or less. In the end, no one can predict which accounts will earn money in a year and which ones will tank. The beauty of starting to save so early is that you have time to be aggressive and make up for any losses because you'll be saving for so long.

The key is to take the plunge and start investing every month. Contact a fee-only financial advisor now.

How to open a retirement account

All it takes to open a retirement account is a completed application, a photo ID, and a blank check. The whole process takes about 5 minutes to complete.

When the companies mail you a prospectus, they will include an application to open your account. If you have any questions feel free to call the customer service line. They will answer any questions you have and walk you through the application.

How to close or change your account

The money is always yours, even when it's in the retirement account. You always have the option of closing your account, moving your account to a different company, and choosing a different account at the same company to invest in. It's best to "rollover" the funds in your account to a different account instead of taking the money our of one account and putting it in another. Taking money out may trigger fees. "Rollingover" your money from one account to another does not trigger fees.

If you want your money back or you want to change your account, call up the company that manages your retirement account and they will send you the correct forms to fill out. Remember, taking money out of a retirement account may trigger penalties. The money is there for use in your old age so try to leave it there.

At the end of the day opening a retirement account and saving for retirement is really easy and is definitely in your best interest. If you think that social security will be there to help take care of your needs in retirement, think again. Visit the social security administration's website located in the Resources section in the back of this book to estimate how much money social security will pay out to you in retirement.

The earlier you start saving the less you have to save. Start saving now.

Tips
> If your employer offers a 401k or 403b retirement plan it's usually best to start saving there. Many employers will "match" funds that you invest up to a set percentage. If you don't sign up and

contribute, you won't get the "match". It's like giving away free money.

➤ Start taking advantage of compound interest by saving as much as you can as soon as you can.

➤ Realize that you have a long time to go before you'll need your retirement money. Contribute steadily and you'll be fine.

➤ Never "close" a retirement account; "roll it over". When you "close" an account the IRS views that as you taking the money out of the account and will levy taxes and penalties. When you "roll it over" the money goes from one institution to the next and no fines or penalties need to be paid.

Shay Olivarria

Chapter Ten

Default

Why you need to have a plan to pay off your student loans

- ➤ Taking out loans
- ➤ Repayment
- ➤ New student loan rules

For many students, student loans will end up being the bane of their existence. The Project on Student Debt estimates that the Class of 2007 graduated with about $20,000 in student loan debt. There are several options available to college students to pay for college costs. The most common are grants, scholarships, and jobs, however when there is a gap between the costs of tuition, books, living, and what you are able to pay for those things many college students turn to student loans.

Taking out loans

Let's be clear: student loans are actual loans that must be paid back *with interest*. There is a practice among college students to take out more money in student loans than they actually need so that they will get a refund check after the semester begins and the tuition, dorms, and books have been paid for. What many students don't think about is that whatever money you take out now a) is accruing interest from the day they give you the loan money b) you will have to pay back c) interest will be tacked on to the principle and will not stop accruing until *all* the money is paid back.

Repayment

Six months after you graduate you'll be expected to start paying the loans back. You'll have to watch the interest rate you're paying and make sure that the loan company, or federal Direct Loan servicing center, has the correct contact information for you. There are different repayment plans, many of them take into account how much money you earn and how much disposable income you have to pay the loans back.

The bottom line is, "You took out the loans. It's your responsibility to pay them back".

New Student Loan Rules

In 2010 some very important things happened to student loans:

#1 Banks were taken out of the business of offering student loans which will save American taxpayers $61 billion over 10 years. Banks have handled the management of federally backed student loans since 1965. While private student loan companies will continue to provide loans, they will no longer be able to offer federally backed loans. Less profit for banks means more money for student grants.

#2 The money the government used to pay banks for "managing" the student loans will now go to the Pell grant program. This means that the average Pell Grant will increase from $4,750 to $5,350. That extra $600 is really going to help students out.

#3 Need-based federal student loan interest rates will get a series of cuts until the rate is 3.4% in 2011. That means that college costs will be manageable again. It will be hard to find a loan rate as low as 3.4% to pay for anything, let alone college costs.

#4 While you're paying back your student loans, the most your payments will be is 15% of your *discretionary* income. That means that no longer will college graduates have to struggle to pay back loans.

#5 Student loans will be completely forgiven if they aren't paid off after 25 years. Imagine that! College graduates that work for non-profits and youth development institutions tend to graduate only to find awesome jobs with mediocre salaries. Now, student loans will be forgiven in time to avoid paying back your student loan debt while you're in retirement.

Tips
- ➢ Only take out as much money in student loans as you actually need.
- ➢ Remember that everything you take out in loans, you'll have to pay back with interest.

Shay Olivarria

Resources

Find out more about credit unions by visiting
www.CreditUnion.coop

Find out current CD rates, mortgage rates, and credit card rates by visiting
www.BankRate.com

Estimate your social security payments by visiting
www.SSA.gov/OACT/QuickCalc/

Locate a Fee-Only Financial Advisor
http://findanadvisor.napfa.org/Home.aspx

Read more about personal finance online at

www.BiggerThanYourBlock.com

Shay Olivarria

Glossary

401k/403b – employer sponsored retirement savings account. Usually, the employer offers a "match" of whatever funds you save up to a specific percentage.

CARD Act – Credit Card Accountability, Responsibility and Disclosure Act of 2009. New legislation that regulates financial institutions offering credit cards.

Compound interest – interest that is added to the principle so that during the next cycle of interest you earn money on both the principle and the interest from last month.

Cooperative economics – working together as a group to make financial gains.

Credit score - the numerical representation of your credit behavior. Range is 300 to 850.

Debt ratio – the number that represents how much of the credit that's been offered to you that's been used.

Disposable/discretionary income – the amount of money that you have left over after you've paid your bills, saved money in your emergency account, and saved for retirement.

Emergency account – money that you have set aside to use specifically for emergencies.

FICO score – the mathematical computation from the Fair Isaac Corporation that puts your financial behavior into a numerical representation. Scores range from 300 – 800.

Financial advisor – a person that helps you create a financial plan. There are several different designations and "types" of financial advisors. Locate a fee-only advisor because they don't sell products so they will be less biased in steering you towards specific products and services.

Hard inquiries – the act of checking your credit reports and/or scores by a third party. For example when you apply for a new credit card or apply for a car loan and the company that you are applying to "runs" your credit. These inquiries stay on your credit report for two years and are considered negative.

Individual Retirement Account (IRA) – retirement savings account that is not sponsored by an employer.

Installment accounts – debt payments that stay the same over time based on the initial agreement. For example a mortgage payment or auto loan payment.

Match – when your employer provides a specific amount of money to your retirement account based on how much money you contribute. Always contribute enough money to get the full match. If you don't, it's like turning down free money.

Mutual fund – an investment account that invests in both stocks and bonds.

Net worth – a true measure of your financial worth. Add up all your assets and subtract all your liabilities (debts) from them. The number that you get is your net worth.

Penalty – when a company and/or government agency requires a monetary payment because of an action initiated by the customer.

Retirement account – an investment account through a 401k/403b or Individual Retirement Account (IRA) that helps you save for retirement by using special tax rules.

Revolving accounts – debt that increases or decreases based on your behavior. For example, credit card bills are higher or lower depending on how much you charge on those cards.

Rollover – the act of moving the money in a retirement account to another retirement account without taking a distribution. No fees or penalties will be levied. If you close an account and the company mails you a check that's a distribution and fines, fees, and/or penalties may apply.

Soft inquiries – the act of viewing your own credit reports and/or scores. You can check your reports and/or scores all day and there will be no negative consequences. Also see "hard inquiries".

Books from Shay Olivarria

All My Mistakes: Money tips for kids in care

10 Things College Students Need to Know About Money

Money Matters: The Get It Done in 1 Minute Workbook

Order books online at www.BiggerThanYourBlock.com

Shay Olivarria

BONUS eBook

I'll Tell You What I Know

(Resumes, interviewing, careers)

By: Shay Olivarria

www.BiggerThanYourBlock.com

I don't know a whole lot of things in the world, but I do know how to get a job. I've put together some tips that I've learned over the years. Take from it what you will.

Resumes

Email addresses

Your email address should always be something neutral, like your name. This is not the place to be creative or attention-grabbing. Also, you need to have *at least* two email addresses. One for personal use (friends, social media registration, etc.). One for business (resumes, business contacts, etc.). A great third one is a "junk mail" that you only use to sign up for newsletters and things you can't opt-out of.

Format

There are two basic formats: chronological and skills-based. Either list your experience from most recent to most current or in order of experience that directly relates to the position. I'm a big fan of skills-based resumes because I don't care what you've done. I care about how your skills relate to the position I need to fill.

Details

No one wants to read a paragraph about your work experience. If they wanted a story, they'd have asked for a curriculum vitae (CV). Use bullet points. Be specific and describe your job responsibilities and *how you added value to your team* in about 4 bullet points. Get to the point, already.

Don't do this
Make sure there are no misspellings or typos. Make sure your job titles, manager's name, and business phone numbers are all correct. Update your address, phone, and, appropriate, email info.

Example:

Toni Stewart
8888 Green Acres Place
Aztlan, CA 90260
(xxx) xxx-xxxx
ToniStewart@shaymail.com

Customer Representative. XYZ Company. Keita Scott. (xxx) xxx-xxxx.
1/2009 – current.
Trained 2 new representatives on GGG software.
Exceeded minimum response goals daily.

Job interviews
Research
Google it. Find out who you'll be interviewing with and check them out on LinkedIn.com. Browse the company's website to learn about the history. Read recent press releases. Know what the company is about and, of possible, what the person interviewing you is about.

Dress appropriately
Wear something conservative. It's better to be overdressed than underdressed. Whether you like it or not people do judge you on how you're dressed. If you're interviewing at a bank, showing all your tattoos, face piercings, and underwear probably won't get you the job. Likewise, if you're interviewing at a tattoo parlor, then showing up in a suit might not be the way to go.

Apply at a job that you think you'll fit in well at. Don't try to fit a square peg into a round hole. Here are some good across-the-board strategies:

Women	Men
No short skirts/tight clothes	No sagging pants
No cleavage	No strong smells (cologne, body odor, etc.)
No heavy make-up	No wrinkled clothes
No strong smells (cologne, body odor, etc.)	No tight clothes
No wrinkled clothes	Wear small/conservative jewelry
Wear small/conservative jewelry	

Be your best self
You don't want to misrepresent yourself, but you do want to show the best version of yourself. Practice interviewing if you have to. The more you can answer

questions about yourself, your skills, and how your experience fits the position with confidence the better you'll do.

Send a thank-you card
Once the interview is over, make sure to send a quick handwritten thank you card. Write something simple like, "thanks for taking the time to meet with me. I look forward to hearing from you soon". Sign your name at the bottom and drop it the mail the same day or the day after you interview. IT sends two messages #1 you're detail-oriented #2 you're thoughtful #3 you're well mannered #4 it will remind the interviewer of your name. Things that are familiar become things we like. Stay top-of-mind.

Career

Have a strategy
Regardless of what job you're applying for, try to get something more from it than just a paycheck. There are valuable skills to be learned at any job. From day one, start thinking about how you can build your transferable skills. With each new position try to have more responsibility, be in a position to learn new skills, interact with more people, and make more money.

Know the difference between a sponsor and a mentor
A sponsor is someone that will advocate for you at your job. A mentor is someone that helps you when you have questions about work. It may seem like a small

difference, but this difference could make or break your career.

Find a sponsor
Having a mentor is awesome. You get to have someone, usually more senior than you in experience, that you can bounce questions off of. This person may help you make decisions or give you advice on a range of career-related topics. That's wonderful, but you need to find a sponsor.

A sponsor is going to suggest you get a plum project, bring up your name in discussions with high-level decision-makers, and encourage you to take one project over another because of the political implications. Top-level people usually respect someone with moxy. If you'd like a particular person to be your sponsor do your research, send out some feelers (you remember asking your crush's best friend if they thought your crush liked you before you approached your crush, right?), and take the initiative to start building a relationship with the person. You need someone, with more pull than you, to speak for you to the right people.

Shay Olivarria is the most dynamic financial education speaker working today, a foster care alumni, and the author of three books on personal finance. She's been quoted at Bankrate.com, FoxBusiness.com, The Credit Union Times, Redbook, and Essence, among others. Book Shay to speak at your event.

www.BiggerThanYourBlock.com.

19895087R00045

Made in the USA
Charleston, SC
17 June 2013